Classrooms
~with a~
Difference

Cameron Macintosh

Classrooms with a Difference

Text: Cameron Macintosh
Publishers: Tania Mazzeo and Eliza Webb
Series consultant: Amanda Sutera
  Hands on Heads Consulting
Editors: Laken Ballinger and Sarah Layton
Project Editor: Annabel Smith
Designer: Leigh Ashforth
Project designer: Danielle Maccarone
Permissions researcher: Catherine Kerstjens
Production controller: Renee Tome

Acknowledgements
We would like to thank the following for permission to reproduce
copyright material:

Front cover, p. 5: Shutterstock.com/Dmytro Zinkevych; pp. 1, 7 (top),
22 (top left): Getty Images/lacaosa; p. 4: iStock.com/JohnnyGreig;
p. 6: Newspix/News Ltd/Wayne Jones; p. 7 (middle): Alamy Stock Photo/
Doug Steley B; pp. 8, 9: Charlotte Curd Photography; pp. 9, 13, 17, 21
(frame edge): stock.adobe.com/Fredex; p. 10 (main): Dreamstime.com/
Michael Deemer, (inset): John Ball Zoo; p. 11 (top): John Ball Zoo, (middle
left): Shutterstock.com/Michael Deemer, (middle right): Alamy Stock
Photo/Michael Deemer; pp. 12 (main), 13, 22 (bottom right), 24: Tsai
Design Studio; p. 12 (inset): Shutterstock.com/EvrenKalinbacak; pp. 14, 15,
22 (top right): Getty Images/Jonas Gratzer; pp. 16, 17: Alamy Stock Photo/
Joerg Boethling; p. 18 (main), back cover: Alamy Stock Photo/paul
prescott; p. 18 (inset): Alamy Stock Photo/Matthew Williams-Ellis; pp. 19,
22 (bottom left): Getty Images/Putu Sayoga; pp. 20, 21: Alamy Stock
Photo/Edmund Sumner-VIEW.

Every effort has been made to trace and acknowledge copyright.
However, if any infringement has occurred, the publishers tender their
apologies and invite the copyright holders to contact them.

NovaStar

Text © 2024 Cengage Learning Australia Pty Limited

Cengage Learning Australia
Level 5, 80 Dorcas Street
Southbank VIC 3006 Australia
Phone: 1300 790 853
Email: aust.nelsonprimary@cengage.com

For learning solutions, visit **cengage.com.au**

Printed in China by 1010 Printing International Ltd
1 2 3 4 5 6 7 28 27 26 25 24

*Nelson acknowledges the Traditional Owners and Custodians
of the lands of all First Nations Peoples. We pay respect
to Elders past and present, and extend that respect to
all First Nations Peoples today.*

Contents

Many Ways to Learn

Learning can take place in all sorts of ways, in all sorts of places. With access to the internet, we can learn from almost anywhere. However, most students go to schools and attend their lessons in a classroom.

An everyday classroom can look like this.

Even a forest can be a classroom.

Although most schools are similar in many ways, some look very unusual or are found in unexpected places. These schools can give their students interesting learning experiences. For example, students who go to a school near a forest can go out into nature and learn about it up close.

But not everyone can go to school in person. Some people live far away from any schools. Others are unable to go to school because they are living in **poverty**. Sometimes, teachers must find clever ways to reach their students.

Online Classrooms

Some schools use technology to connect teachers with students living in **remote** areas. This is known as a "School of the Air". Children in many parts of Australia learn through a School of the Air.

The first School of the Air began in 1951 in Alice Springs, a remote town in Australia's Northern Territory. Students used **shortwave radios** to listen to their lessons from home.

Children do their schoolwork via radio at home in 1984.

Students can now use tablets or computers for remote learning.

Today, most of these schools run online classes for an hour each day. Students can see and talk to their teachers, as well as other students, on computer screens. After their lessons, they continue their schoolwork with help from their parents or other carers.

In remote places, a satellite dish is used to connect to the internet.

Think and Discuss

Would you enjoy doing all of your schoolwork online? Why or why not?

7

Nature as a Classroom

Green School in Taranaki, Aotearoa New Zealand, was built to bring students closer to nature. The school is near a forest, some mountains and a river.

Many of the school's buildings are made from natural materials, such as wood from pine trees. Some buildings are shaped like **seed pods** with large windows to give students views of the surrounding nature.

The classrooms at Green School are surrounded by nature.

The teachers at Green School plan lessons that make use of the school's natural environment. For example, students might study water from the nearby river as part of their science lessons. They also learn about how to care for nature, and they can take part in **reforestation** projects in their local area.

Students learn about how plants grow at Green School.

Think and Discuss

Why do you think a pod shape was chosen for some of the school's buildings?

A Classroom Inside a Zoo

Every year in Michigan, USA, a group of students do their studies at Zoo School. This school is located inside John Ball Zoo, which is home to a wide range of animals.

Zoo School is located in John Ball Zoo.

Zoo staff can teach students a lot about animals and their habitats.

Zoo School students learn the same things as students at other schools, but the zoo is often a part of their lessons. For example, they might have some classes on the zoo grounds or learn how the zookeepers care for the animals.

Students can study in Zoo School's forest classroom.

Students can see red pandas and lemurs at John Ball Zoo.

Think and Discuss

What would you most like to learn about if you were a student at Zoo School?

A Classroom Inside a Shipping Container

The Vissershok Container Classroom is part of the Vissershok Primary School near Cape Town, South Africa. The classroom was built out of a recycled shipping container – a large metal box that was used to transport items on ships. A shipping container was chosen for the classroom because it was **inexpensive** and could be used in different ways.

shipping containers on a ship

Vissershok Container Classroom

In the morning, students come inside for their classes. Then, in the afternoon, the classroom is used as the school's library.

A door and windows have been cut into the sides of the container, and a roof has been added. The gap between the container and the roof helps keep the classroom cool. The classroom also has a vegetable garden outside where students can learn to grow food.

The open roof of the shipping container classroom lets in cool air.

Think and Discuss Why would it be important to keep the shipping container classroom cool?

Boat Schools

In Bangladesh, the **monsoon** season between June and October is a time of heavy rain and wind. It can cause flooding in many areas of the country. The floods then prevent children in these areas from getting to school. A fleet, or group, of classroom boats was set up so that these children could continue their education.

Children leave their boat school in Bangladesh after finishing their lessons.

These boats travel along riverbanks to pick up students near their homes. The boats then **dock** in a safe place, and teachers give their lessons. Afterwards, the boats take the students back to where they boarded, and the students can return to their homes.

Children listen to their teacher on board a boat school.

Think and Discuss

How might your learning be affected if it was very difficult for you to get to school?

Train Station Schools

In the state of Odisha in India, teachers have been giving classes for children on train station **platforms** since 1985. The children sit on the station platforms and learn as trains and passengers go by. Many of the children who go to these classes are homeless, which means they live on the streets. The school gives them four hours of lessons a day, as well as health education.

A group of children attend a train station school in Mumbai, India.

Doing schoolwork on the floor is tricky, but it gives this boy a chance to learn.

When the idea began, classes were held at only one train station. The school helped so many children that since then, more railway platform schools have been set up throughout the country.

Think and Discuss

Apart from going to school, what other challenges might homeless children have?

A School in a Jungle

There is a Green School on the island of Bali, in Indonesia. This school is located in a jungle and is a **sustainable** school. The school buildings are made mostly from bamboo, a type of plant that is easy to find in the jungle and grows back quickly after being cut down. The school gets its power from **solar panels**.

a bamboo forest

Green School in Bali has open-air classrooms made from bamboo.

Students at Green School learn a lot about caring for Earth. One way they do this is by helping the school run its own **recycling centre**. Students also work in the school's gardens by growing fruits and vegetables, which they eat together.

A student makes recycled paper with a teacher at Green School in Bali.

Think and Discuss

What are some ways your school is sustainable?

A School Without Walls

Fuji Yōchien (say: *foo-jee yoh-chi-en*) is a kindergarten in Tokyo, Japan. It was built in the shape of an oval with an open space in the middle. There are no walls between the classrooms, and the doors to the outside are left open most of the year. Trees poke through the school's circular roof **deck** and even into some of the classrooms.

Fuji Yōchien Kindergarten

Students at Fuji Yōchien are given a lot more freedom than students at most other schools. They can play on the roof deck, and they can even use the school's trees to climb to their classrooms!

A tree leads from one level of the school to another.

Children play on the circular roof deck at Fuji Yōchien.

Think and Discuss

Would you enjoy going to a school like Fuji Yōchien? Why?

Learning Can Happen Anywhere

All of these schools help students to learn about the world around them while they do their lessons. These schools show that learning can happen in many different places, in lots of interesting ways.

Glossary

deck (*noun*) — a wooden floor built outside

dock (*verb*) — when a boat stops and stays in one place

inexpensive (*adjective*) — not costing much money

monsoon (*noun*) — a heavy rain in South Asia that usually comes in summer

platforms (*noun*) — parts of a train station where trains stop to let people on and off

poverty (*noun*) — not having enough money for basic needs, such as food, housing or clothing

recycling centre (*noun*) — a place where waste materials are sorted and reused

reforestation (*noun*) — the act of planting new trees in places where forests have been cut down

remote (*adjective*) — far away from other people and towns

seed pods (*noun*) — parts of plants that contain seeds

shortwave radios (*noun*) — types of radios used for communication

solar panels (*noun*) — devices that use the heat and light from the Sun to make electricity

sustainable (*adjective*) — not harmful to the environment

Index